Contents

First
published 2004 by Walker
Books Limited, 87 Vauxhall Walk
London SE11 5HJ 10 9 8 7 6 5 4 3 2 1
Text © 2004 Jeanne Willis Illustrations © 2004
Lydia Monks Printed in China All rights reserved
This book has been typeset in Clichee and Tree
No part of this book may be reproduced, transmitted
or stored in an information retrieval system in any form
or by any means, graphic, electronic or mechanical, including
photocopying, taping and recording, without prior written
permission from the publisher British Library Cataloguing
in Publication data: a catalogue record for this book
is available from the British Library
ISBN 0-7445-8683-6

WALKER BOOKS
AND SUBSIDIARIES
LONDON · BOSTON · SYDNEY · AUCKLAND

www.walkerbooks.co.uk

Part One

Soulmates

'Cos a girl's
best friend isn't
always a
diamond.

WHAT ARE FRIENDS FOR?

There comes a time in every girl's life when she realizes that while her aged parents offer a fantastic taxi service, their taste in music sucks, their idea of a good night out is a dull night in and they look sad when they dance. This is why we need mates. Friends v. Parents? No contest!

What parents say

You can't go out looking like that!

Call this music?

Put a coat on – it's snowing.

What time do you call this?

Let's go to the zoo!

You can't possibly walk in those!

Take that muck off your face!

Have you finished your homework?

You treat this place like a hotel.

Would you like some lemonade?

All you do is watch the telly.

That's not good for you!

4

What friends say

Love that miniskirt with those thigh boots!

Man, these lyrics are so deep.

Why bother wearing spaghetti straps if no one's going to see them?

What? It's only 3 in the morning!

Let's go skinny-dipping in the boys' pool.

5-inch stilettos! Can I borrow them, *pleease*?

Great lippy!

Have you finished with your bloke?

Everybody round to my place!

Vodka and cherryade, anyone?

Come round and watch the vid of us at that party we crashed.

Have you got a light, mate?

Q Help! I'm confused – I don't know who I am, what I want or who to hang out with any more.

When you were little, you just wanted to be a princess – life was so simple! Then you grew up. Now your body and mind keep changing and it can feel like you don't know "you" any more. To make things harder, everyone else is telling you what to do, what to think and even what to wear. But hang on – this is your personality, not theirs! The "true you" is a unique combo of different things that are constantly changing. A good way of finding out what makes you tick is to experiment. Change your hair, try new activities. Go to new places and meet new people – you've got your whole lifetime to discover yourself.

looks

Some stuff that makes you YOU.

1. Your looks

2. Your style

likes

3. Your likes and dislikes

4. Your beliefs

5. Your interests

talents

6. Your talents and weaknesses

7. Your voice and the things you say

8. Your sense of humour

9. How you treat people

ambitions

10. Your ambitions

GET THIS!

"Friendship with oneself is all-important because without it, one cannot be friends with anyone else in the world." (Eleanor Roosevelt)

Q Help! I've got blonde hair – everyone assumes I'm dumb.

It isn't just clothes that come with labels – it's people too. We're all guilty of judging each other on appearance. Great if your label says "Intelligent superbabe", but a real bummer if it's screaming "Blonde bimbo" just because of your hair colour. There are loads of dumb assumptions people make without bothering to get to know you. Why? They're basically ignorant, jealous ... or just rude. It's embarrassing and hurtful, but don't take it personally – it says more about them than it does about you.

Labels you should ignore:

GIRLS WHO WEAR GLASSES: geek, swot, goody-goody

PRETTY GIRLS: thick, vain, shallow

GIRLS WHO AREN'T INTERESTED IN BOYS, MAKE-UP AND CLOTHES: dyke, butch

GIRLS WHO ARE BIG: stupid, greedy, lazy

GIRLS WHO ARE VERY SLIM: anorexic, neurotic

GIRLS WITH BIG BOOBS: slut, flirt, freak

GIRLS WHO DRESS DIFFERENTLY: weirdo, loser

What to do if you've been wrongly labelled:

1. Don't bottle it up. Talking to girls in a similar situation might give you some tips.

2. Learn how to deal with your reaction to stupid comments. Anyone who says nasty things clearly has a problem – pity them!

3. Educate people – they may be using words that are offensive now, but weren't in the past. Explain what you prefer to be called, politely but firmly.

4. Don't "become" your label by believing in a nasty comment made years ago. Make a list of all your good points and hold on to positive feelings about yourself.

Q Help! I'd like to make new friends but I'm really shy.

There's nothing worse than thinking you are going to make a complete dork of yourself in public; going bright red, not knowing what to say, saying the wrong thing or being rejected are things we all dread. Shyness can be conquered, though – here are some ways:

1 Imagine you've known the person you're talking to for years.

2 Smile! You'll look friendly and approachable, even if you're shaking in your stilettos.

3 If you have to walk into a room full of people, imagine they're sitting on the loo – they'll seem far less scary.

4 Plan what to say in advance. Find out what people are into. If it's horses, don't say "Do you like horses?", in case they just nod. Say "You know lots about horses... Could I ask you something about them?"

5 Remember that everyone isn't looking at you – you're not the Queen.

6 If you're not a great talker, be a great listener. Show you're interested by asking questions: "Really? Then what happened?"

7 Look confident – chin up, shoulders relaxed, back straight. Look people in the eye, and if your hands are shaking, put them behind your back.

8 Keep saying "I'm in charge!" to yourself, like you're the boss. After all, why should you feel inferior to the other person?

9 If someone says "hi", don't just say "hi" back – offer them a chip, ask if they want to join in, pay them a compliment... Anything to show you want to be friends.

10 Join in! Do activities where you'll meet people who are into the same stuff – that's when friendships happen naturally.

IT TAKES ALL SORTS

Some girls like to hang out in a crowd, some like to have one best friend and others prefer to pic 'n' mix. While each friend is unique, they tend to fit certain categories – so where do your mates fit in?

BESTEST MATE: You're soul-sisters who like the same things. You're so close, you tell each other everything – including the truth!

OLD CHUMS: You go way back! You were both sheep in the school nativity. You don't see each other much, but when you do, it's like you've never been apart.

PONY PALS/BALLET BUDDIES: Friends who share the same activities. When you are together you're as close as anything, but you don't go out of your way to meet up.

FAKE FRIENDS: They look like sweet mermaids but they're fishing for something and just pretend to like you till they get it. Avoid!

MUM'S MATE: A girl your mum thinks you should invite over for tea ... but why? (You don't tell *her* who to play with!)

DIVA: Leader of the in-crowd. You only hang out with her to make yourself look cool. Everyone's scared of her, but deep down she's a bit sad – she's got no real mates.

GIRL PACK: These are the girls you call on when your bezzy mate has fallen out with you or been grounded. You like each other lots and hang out at school in a boy-scaring bunch.

FAIR-WEATHER FRIEND: This girl just wants to have fun. She'll share the good times, but if you're having a bad time, you won't see her for dust.

MONA-LENA: A walking crisis, she has to lean on people or she falls over. If you have the patience to adopt her, you'll be rewarded with puppy-like affection.

Q Help! My so-called best mate told me I had BO – should I forgive her?

Depends how she told you. If she climbed on the school roof and shouted it through a megaphone, cross her off your Christmas card list now! If, however, she took you

Good Mates OR

Good mates don't mind you having boyfriends

Good mates keep secrets

Good mates let you cry

Good mates help you up

Good mates let you go first

Good mates listen

Good mates laugh with you

Good mates say sorry

Good mates are giving

Good mates stick together

It's my last one but YOU can have it.

aside and whispered, "Listen, mate – not sure your deodorant's working properly," she's done you a favour. Say thanks. Surely it's better to hear the truth from your best friend rather than go round minging? It might have hurt, but she has your best interests at heart.

Bad Mates?

Bad mates have your boyfriends.

Bad mates spread gossip.

Bad mates make you cry.

Bad mates let you down.

Bad mates let you go.

Bad mates are too busy talking.

Bad mates laugh at you.

Bad mates forgive no one.

Bad mates only take.

Bad mates tear you apart.

Blah blah blah... Did you say something?

Q Help! My parents don't like my friends – what can I do?

Parents always fear the worst – it's their job. When you refuse to bring your mates home, they naturally assume you must be hanging out with hookers or hooligans. If you don't tell them all the good things about your friends, parents are forced to

What your parents see:

Long black hair **+** long black clothes **+** Doc Martens = KATIE WORSHIPS SATAN

Sexy clothes **+** make-up **+** heels = MANDY IS A SLUT, AN UNMARRIED MOTHER

Pale skin **+** slim and grungy = KARA'S A DRUG ADDICT LIVING IN A SQUAT

Cool boy **+** bling **+** money = KELVIN IS A DRUG DEALER, PIMP

make snap judgements about them based on brief, doorstep encounters. Little wonder they leap to the wrong conclusions. Try seeing it from their point of view, then put them straight. This is what your charming, intelligent friends look like from where Mum and Dad are standing:

What they're really like:

Katie is a blood donor. Her mum works as a costumier and makes all her clothes.

Mandy's a cheerleader. She's raised loads for the Children's Hospital.

Kara's a dancer – she's just got a grant for the Russian Ballet School.

Kelvin got 98% in Humanities and wants to be a vicar like his dad.

LOSING A FRIEND

Sadly, although we'd love to be friends for ever, it isn't always the case. Friends fall out. Or they move away. Hardest of all to bear is when a friend dies. It's only natural to be sad, to miss them and to think that life will never be as good again. But remember, although no one can ever replace your friend, the world is full of potential new best mates, all with their own lovable ways. When you find each other – and she or he could be just round the corner – the friend you've lost will become a wonderful memory.

You'll never forget her, but one day you'll find yourself feeling happy thinking about the good times you had together, and the awful hurt will fade.

Part Two

Sex & Snogs

What's really going on in boys' brains (and down their boxers!)

Q How come girls have such a tough time growing up and boys don't?

But they do! Boys might not have to worry about their bra size or the price of tampons, but they've got plenty of other reasons to get their boxers in a twist. Lots of weird mind and body stuff is happening to them too. If anything, it's harder for them because they'd rather be skinned alive than discuss personal problems with their mates. They suffer alone. So if you see one, be gentle – chances are, he's having an even worse time than you.

THINGS BOYS WORRY ABOUT

Their voices breaking

Being spotty and smelly

Their weight

Their height

Embarrassing erections

Sex – doing it wrong, not doing it at all, having no one to do it with

Crying in public

The size of their willy

Being a loser

Nobody fancying them

Not being cool

Being bullied

Not fitting in

Being laughed at by girls

Being gay

Screwing up in front of their mates

Being crap at sport

HOW BOYS CHANGE
AT PUBERTY

Boys usually hit puberty when they're about 13, but it can begin any time between 10 and 18. It starts when a hormone called testosterone is released into their bodies – this kick-starts their testicles into making sperm and triggers off all sorts of changes that will eventually turn them into fully-fledged blokes.

face shape alters

moustache

deep voice

taller

1 THEY GROW TALLER (so they can get rude magazines off the top shelf).

2 FACE SHAPE ALTERS (so they look old enough to get into X-rated movies).

3 MOUSTACHE AND BEARD BEGIN TO GROW (so they nick your razor).

4 VOICE GETS DEEPER (so they can get out of choir).

5 SHOULDERS AND CHEST GET BROADER (so they can carry your shopping).

6 PUBIC HAIR AND UNDERARM HAIR GROWS (so how come they never wax?).

7 PENIS AND TESTICLES GET BIGGER (so they fill their boxers).

8 SPERM IS MADE IN TESTICLES (so they can make babies – watch out!).

beard

broader chest

hair grows

GET THIS!

On average, boys reach puberty later than girls.

Q Which planet do boys come from?

It has been said that we're from Venus and they're from Mars, but boys aren't aliens really. Once you get to know them, you'll find they're human after all. Here are some of the exciting varieties:

1. FOOTY FAN: He lives for Match of the Day. If you stood stark naked in front of the telly he'd tell you to move in case he missed a goal. His team is his tribe.

2. JOHNNY REBEL: He's cool, he's mean, he's moody. Very moody – it's like PMT! If only he wasn't so good-looking...

3. CLASS CLOWN: If you fancy this one, your best bet is to laugh at his jokes. Don't tell your own or he'll walk off the stage.

4. ARTY FARTY: A deep thinker who deeply thinks he's misunderstood. Nobody

understands him, so don't even try.

5. BOY NEXT DOOR: You used to play in his paddling pool as kids. But somewhere along the line, he turned into Brad Pitt!

6. MR POPULAR: Cute but cool. Mature and very clever – he'll be a sexy lawyer or a doctor one day. Hard to get to, this one.

7. SHY GUY: He might be seriously lush but he's already decided you'll reject him, so you have to make the first move.

8. GEEK: His head's always in a book, but somehow his weird genius turns you on. If you want him, you'll have to swot up.

9. ACTION MAN: First you have to catch him! Put on your PE kit and knock his sports sox off!

10. CAMP DAVID: He acts gay but probably isn't. Who cares? – a man who actively begs you to come shopping!

Q Help! I get on really well with this lad from school, but when he's with his mates he just blanks me.

When boys are with their friends, they turn into different people (or animals). This is perfectly normal, and once you understand it you'll stop taking it personally.

Why boys behave like gorillas when they're with their mates

✪ They love to be part of a gang – it's to do with hunting woolly mammoths together during prehistoric times.

✪ They are secretly scared of girls – they haven't sussed us out yet.

✪ Boys get the mick taken if they admit to liking a girl – which is why they diss you in front of their mates. When the leader gets a girlfriend then suddenly it's OK to have a relationship.

✪ Boys hate to lose at anything – which is why they go ape during footy matches and why they always have to have the loudest burp.

✪ They talk differently when they're with their mates – it's a code made up of grunts that binds them together. Uh? Yuh. Sorted!

✪ They brag and exaggerate (and lie) to their mates about everything in order to be seen as the coolest/sexiest/toughest.

She was **gagging** for it!!!

GET THIS!

On average, girls learn to talk earlier than boys.

Q My friends say I'm pretty, but boys don't seem to fancy me. What am I doing wrong?

Nothing, probably – maybe they're the wrong kind of boys! But just in case, check you're not guilty of committing a typical girly-crime that turns boys off.

12 THINGS GIRLS DO THAT BOYS HATE:

1. Go to the toilet together

2. Wear weird clothes and too much make-up

3. Laugh like donkeys to get attention

BRAY ha hah ha, BRAY ha hah ha!

4. Spend hours getting ready

5. Cry in public

6. Act dumb

7. Agree with everything he says

8. Treat him like a kid

9. Discuss his secrets with their mates

10. Stalk him

11. Show him up in public

12. Keep asking, "Do you love me?"

GET THIS!

In conversations, most girls want to know "Why?" while most boys want to know "How?"

Q How can you tell if a boy fancies you or not?

The last thing he's going to do is tell you, in case you laugh, tell your mates or suggest he takes a running jump. If he teases you, gives you a nickname or kicks your chair away, he probably fancies you rotten; but mostly he'll tell you via his body language. Here are some dead giveaways...

BOY BODY LANGUAGE
FOR
"I FANCY YOU"

* Furtive glances

* Sneaky smiles

* Acting cool

* Showing off

Look at
ME!

* Copying the way you sit

* Touching his hair

* Eye contact

* Being horrible

HOW TO SAY

"I FANCY YOU"

BACK

✳ Flutter your eyelashes (but don't overdo it or you'll just look mental).

✳ Hold his gaze for a few secs, then look away.

✳ Smile back mysteriously.

✳ Tell your mate to tell his mate to tell him.

✳ Lend him your best pen in Geography.

✳ Give him your last chip.

✳ Stand on a chair with a rose between your teeth (ha ha!).

✳ Flick your hair.

Q Help! I'm really shy with boys – I don't know how to talk to them.

The main thing is to be yourself – if you're not sure who that is yet, here are some ways of behaving that boys like:

💜 Listen to him and look interested.

💜 Ask his advice.

❤ Be happy – he won't want to hang out with a whinger.

❤ Make him laugh.

❤ Stand up straight, walk with confidence (you're a princess!).

❤ Praise him! Cheer if he scores or tell him he was robbed if he loses.

❤ Find out what he's into and talk to him about it.

❤ Be mysterious – he doesn't want to know about the boil on your bum.

I've squeezed it but it just won't go!

Q I fancy a boy I play tennis with. I know he *likes* me, but he won't make the first move – is it OK for me to ask him out?

If he won't play ball but fancies the frilly pants off you, go for it. Here's some tips:

1. Pick your moment. Don't ask him to "play doubles" in front of his mates or he might just smack you round the head with his racket – no score.

2. Keep it casual – as in "Fancy going to the pictures/bungee jumping/up the chippy later?" (The ball is now in his court.)

3. If he says "no", stay cool and say that a load of you were going anyway. Don't beg or cry – there'll be other ace players.

4. If he says "yes", don't wrap your arms and legs round him and give him a big, wet kiss – look like it happens every day and ask when he's free. Game, set and match!

First date tips

He's asked you out, he's lush, and the last thing you want to do is blow it. But is that spinach on your teeth? Check out this list...

BEFORE YOU GO

☐ ARE YOU WEARING SCARY CLOTHES? (Boys don't mind other girls looking crazy or tarty – but not their dates.)

☐ HAVE YOU REMEMBERED TO WEAR DEODORANT?

☐ IS YOUR BREATH FRESH? (Carry mints/breath fresheners with you.)

☐ HAVE YOU GOT SCUM/LIPSTICK/FOOD ON YOUR TEETH?

☐ IS YOUR MAKE-UP OTT? (Do you look like a drag queen?)

☐ HAVE YOU GOT A BOGEY UP YOUR NOSE?

☐ IS YOUR SKIRT CAUGHT IN YOUR KNICKERS? (Look at your rear view in the mirror.)

☐ ARE YOU WEARING YOUR BEST UNDERWEAR? (Grey bra straps are grim.)

☐ ARE YOU WEARING TOO MUCH PERFUME? (A light mist only – it's not flyspray.)

ON THE DATE...

If you don't fancy him, at least be kind – say thank you and a quick bye.

Turn up on time and remember his name – don't call him Kevin if it's Colin.

Meet somewhere neutral so your dad can't give him the Spanish Inquisition.

If you bump into his mates, be friendly and sr sweetly but don't get clingy.

Tell him he looks nice – he'll have made an effort, even if it doesn't show.

If there's a ghastly silence, ask him about something he's into and make it so he can't just answer yes or no. Hopefully it'll get a conversation going.

If he hugs you and you want him to kiss yor look him in the eye – bo usually read that as encouragement.

Offer to pay your way, but if he insists on paying, let him.

KNOW A GOOD DATE FROM A BAD ONE

🙂 He missed the cup final for you.

🙂🙂 He's had a tattoo of your name.

🙂🙂 He sucked off your indelible lipstick.

🙂🙂🙂 He gave you his grandma's engagement ring.

🙂🙂 He cried when you left.

🙁 You fell asleep while he was talking.

🙁🙁 He brought his mum with him.

🙁🙁 He said he fancied your best mate.

🙁🙁🙁 His girlfriend turned up and hit you with her handbag.

🙁🙁🙁 He made you feel small, ugly and stupid.

HOW TO DUMP HIM

You're **DUMPED,** sucker!

"Breaking up is hard to do", according to ancient but very accurate lyrics. If you know you've come to the end of the line with a guy, it's not easy to tell him, especially if he's done nothing wrong and thinks everything is rosy. If he's been a complete creep and has done something hideous, you're allowed to tell him to get stuffed through a megaphone in the high street. But if you've just stopped loving him, do it gently. There are several ways...

✓ Go to a neutral location and tell him straight: you don't think this is working out; you need space; it's not him, it's you ... anything to cushion the blow.

✓ If you really can't face him, grab your pen and write him a letter.

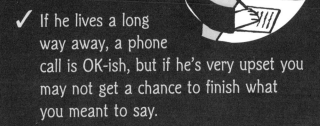

✓ If he lives a long way away, a phone call is OK-ish, but if he's very upset you may not get a chance to finish what you meant to say.

✗ Don't text or e-mail the big heave-ho. If he's been bad, fine. If not, it can come across as cold and uncaring. Don't add insult to injury.

✗ Don't get one of your gozzy mates to tell him – how humiliating is that?!

✓ If he won't take no for an answer, change your mobile number, be "out" when he calls round and let it slip that you have a new (very large) boyfriend.

Worst Case Scenario

HELP! My boyfriend's dumped me. I love him soooo much. How can I ever get over him?

OUCH, it hurts! You thought you meant everything to him and you still don't know where you went wrong. Was it

Action plan

1. GET HIM OUT OF YOUR SYSTEM

❤ Close the curtains, play "your song", lie on the bed and cry and cry. Do not look in the mirror.

❤ Run a bath and relax with chocolate.

❤ Go to bed. Tomorrow is the first day of the rest of your life.

2. GET ANGRY WITH HIM

❤ Stamp on his photo. Tear up his letters and throw them in the bin.

❤ Write a list of all his faults – nobody's

something you did or said? The way you look? Being dumped can leave you feeling like the most unlovable person on the planet. But hang on! This is one guy's opinion. You might look like crap now because you've been crying, but you've had a relationship with someone. He fancied you! Which means you *are* lovable and attractive. Being dumped doesn't have to mean there's something wrong with you – it's the relationship that was wrong. What you need now is a plan of action...

perfect. See him for what he was!

3. GET OVER HIM

❤ Spoil yourself! Get your hair done, buy a new top and some new make-up.

❤ Ring your best mate and make plans.

❤ Go out, have fun – and forget him!

NB It can take time to mend a broken heart, depending on your situation. If the sadness is going on for too long and you can't cope, see your doctor – she knows how to help.

Q Help! My date said he'd call but that was over a week ago!

If he likes you, he'll call, but give him at least a fortnight – he won't want to lose his cool by seeming too keen. If he doesn't ring, he may have taken your number out of politeness – it's kinder than telling a girl she's not his type. No matter how desperate you feel, don't sit by the phone. Go out, have fun! If you're not in when he calls, he'll think you're dead popular and he'll hunt you down!

Q I went to see a boy band and the *lead singer* winked at me. I *love* him so much, I can't stop crying.

Too much hanky and no panky can be truly upsetting. Having a crush on a celeb is so normal, even your nan had one. It's good for working out which kind of guy you fancy, but the chances of you walking down the aisle with him are pretty slim, painful as that seems. Is he really the boy for you? You haven't a clue what he's like as a person. Dance to his music but don't waste your tears on him!

Q I don't want a boyfriend yet – am I abnormal?

No! Nobody "needs" a boyfriend and happiness does not depend on having one. The whole point of hanging out with boys is for fun, but if you've got lots of other fun things to do right now, keep doing 'em! If and when you decide to have a relationship, you'll be a much more interesting person for it. Besides, being single means you're always free to see your mates, no one can be unfaithful to you and you can flirt with whoever you like!

Q What's a *lesbian*?

It's a girl who finds girls sexually attractive instead of boys. However, many girls with boyfriends fantasize about sex with other girls – it's human nature to be curious. Understanding your own sexuality can be confusing, especially when you're young. While some people know for sure that they're "gay" or "straight", loads of us hover in-between.

Eeny, meeny, miney, mo...

LESBIAN (HOMOSEXUAL, GAY, DYKE): A girl who only fancies girls.

BI-CURIOUS: Someone who'd like to get physical with someone of the same sex to see what it's like.

BISEXUAL: Someone who fancies people of both sexes.

HETEROSEXUAL: Someone who fancies people of the opposite sex.

Q Why are some people gay?

Nobody knows for sure. Some think it's genetic – you are either born gay or you're not. Some think it's to do with upbringing and that something in your life makes you "decide" to be gay. Others reckon it's a combination of factors – there's no real proof either way. We're all attracted to different people, and who we fancy may be more to do with our partner's personality than whether they are male or female.

Q What's homophobia?

It means being frightened of, or not liking, homosexuals. Some people think being gay is "unnatural" or "a sin against God". There are even a few intolerant sickos who beat gay people up (queer-bashing). So should you admit you're gay, or not? Some think you should come "out" and be proud. Others think that what you do in private is nobody else's business. In the end, it's down to the individual. Sadly, some gay people feel so ashamed, they commit suicide. This is never, ever the answer. They deserve the same love and respect as straight people. If you're gay and having a tough time, there are plenty of like-minded people who understand and can help. Call them. (See page 80 for a helpline.)

Q Help! I've got a boyfriend but I don't know how to kiss him!

The usual advice is to "do what comes naturally" – bad advice if that means clamping your lips onto his nose or using your tongue like a windscreen-wiper. If your boy hasn't passed his kissing exams either, he may lunge and suck your contact lens out by accident or clamp you by the bottom lip until it goes blue. Don't despair – there is an art to kissing. Pucker up and practise!

How to kiss for beginners

OK, here we go. Put one arm round his waist and the other on his shoulder, or both round his shoulders (not his throat!).

1. Hold him close, then make eye contact.

2. Place your slightly opened mouth lightly against his. (No sudden movements.)

3. Move your mouth slightly in time with his. (Slowly – you're not a goldfish!)

4. Remember to breathe through your nose – bulgy eyes isn't a good look. Close them if you want.

5. Gently suck his lips with yours if you like – but don't make like you're vacuuming the hall.

6. If you use your tongue, be subtle – give him a kiss, not a tonsillectomy.

7. If you dribble, burp or gag, make a joke of it.

Q Help! I missed the sex video at school, so I'm a bit behind on boys' dangly bits.

Boys all have the same basic equipment, but like girls, they come in many shapes and sizes. The biggest difference between boys and us is that they wear their major baby-making equipment on the outside – show-offs!

BOYS' BITS

1. TESTICLES (balls, nuts, knackers, bollocks): These make male sex cells, called sperm.

2. SCROTUM (ball bag, nad sack): Loose pouch of wrinkled skin which hangs outside body and contains testicles.

3. EPIDIDYMIS: Coiled tube where sperm mature. Links testicle to sperm duct.

4. SPERM DUCTS: Carry sperm towards the penis.

5. SEMINAL VESICLES: Glands producing fluid that gives sperm energy.

6. PROSTATE GLAND: Produces fluid which helps sperm move.

7. URETHRA: Carries urine and sperm (but not at the same time).

8. PENIS (willy, knob, cock, dick, prick): Small and soft until sexually excited, then it grows, becomes stiff (erect) and stands away from the body, allowing it to fit into a vagina during sex.

9. GLANS (bell end, helmet): Tip of the penis – the most sensitive part.

10. FORESKIN: Fold of skin that covers glans. Glands underneath produce white creamy stuff called smegma. This helps the skin slide smoothly over the glans. It can get very smelly if not washed regularly. Sometimes the foreskin is removed for religious or medical reasons (called circumcision).

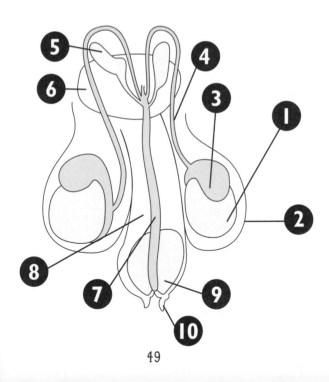

The Great Big Willy page

Q How big is the average willy?

Rulers ready? When the average penis is soft and floppy (flaccid) it measures about 6–10 cm long. When it's erect, it's 12–17 cm long and 3–4 cm thick.

Q What's an erection?

A stiff penis (or "hard-on", in boy-speak). Willies are made of body tissue full of blood vessels. When a boy is turned on, blood pumps into the vessels and his penis goes hard and stands up. Erections can happen at any time – they're not always caused by sexy thoughts. This can be deeply embarrassing if it's unwanted, so do the ladylike thing and pretend not to notice – the boy can't help it.

Q What's ejaculation?

When semen (spunk) squirts out of an erect penis. Semen contains a cocktail of sperm and fluid and there's usually about a teaspoonful each time. It can be any shade from greyish to white to yellow, and when it comes out, it's warm. Ejaculation happens during an orgasm (when he comes/has a climax), usually when the penis is stimulated through sex or masturbation (see pages 56–57). During orgasm, muscles round the bladder tighten so that no urine can come out with the semen.

Q My virgin boyfriend's got a spot on his willy – why?

Genitals get spots and rashes just like faces and they usually go away on their own. Warts are different – they can be caught by having sex with someone who's got them, but virgin boys can get them too. They should see a doctor for treatment.
NB Un-treated genital warts can be passed on to girls through sex and may cause cervical cancer later on.

Wart do you think it is???

What's its name?

Boys love their dick as much as their dog – they stroke it, pet it and, yes, they even give it a name. Here are some of the most common ones:

Knob

Dick

Willy

Chopper

John Thomas

Winkle

Percy

Whanger

Sausage

Prick

Tool

Todger

Cock

Shlong

Truncheon

Dong

AND NOW: A LOAD OF BALLS

From puberty, sperm forms continuously in the testicles – which is why guys old enough to be your grandpa can still become daddies! They are the most sensitive part of the male body – to be knocked in the knackers is the most excruciating of pains (we'll never know, will we ladies?). Boys often worry that one testicle is bigger or hangs lower than the other, but hardly anyone has a truly matching pair.

Q What is a wet dream?

This is when boys ejaculate in their sleep. If it's going to happen (and it doesn't always) it's usually around the age of 12–15. It can come as a shock if they don't know what's going on, and lots of boys think they've wet themselves or that there's something wrong with their dick. But it's just nature's way of getting rid of excess sperm.

Q Is semen poisonous?

No – you could have it on toast if you wanted, but be aware that you can get STDs (sexually transmitted diseases) from semen if your partner is infected.

Hold onto your knicker elastic, girls ...
here comes

THE *SEXY* SECTION

Q Help! When I see a boy I fancy, I feel all tingly inside.

When your sex hormones start working, you become aware of new sensations in your mind and body. Here are some feelings you might experience:

✪ Boys who you used to find gross suddenly seem ... cute!

✪ Your knees turn to jelly when a certain boy walks past.

✪ You find yourself staring at boys when you go swimming.

✪ You suddenly feel shy with a boy you've played with since nursery.

✪ You get a crush on someone in a band and want to have all his babies.

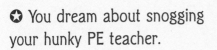

✪ You dream about snogging your hunky PE teacher.

✪ You get butterflies when someone you fancy smiles at you.

✪ You have a desperate urge to be kissed and touched – all over!

✪ You can't stop thinking about someone you fancy.

✪ You don't know whether you want to cry or laugh.

Q Help! sometimes I have really sexy dreams about boys I don't know.

Great, isn't it? Everyone has them, don't worry! Lie back and enjoy. The good thing about sexy dreams and fantasies is that you can do whatever you like with whoever you want and nobody gets hurt.

Q What's masturbation?

Masturbation (wanking, tossing off) is when you touch your genitals for pleasure and sexual relief. Most people do it, each in their own sweet way, often until they have an orgasm (see page 57). Even animals do it. Masturbation doesn't make you go blind or harm you in any way. In fact, it's a good way of getting to know yourself. It's only a problem if you become obsessed and don't do anything else! (But the same could be said for stamp-collecting.)

How girls do it:

Some girls rub their clitoris and/or insert a penis-like object into their vagina (finger, vibrator, etc.). Others use water from a shower-head to tickle their fancy – the possibilities are endless.

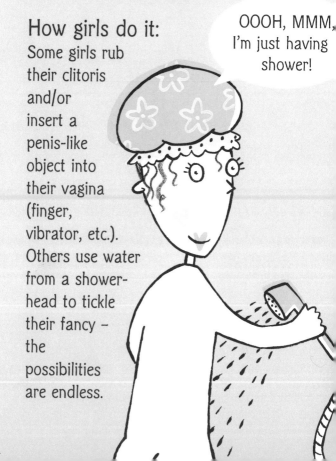

OOOH, MMM, I'm just having shower!

There are two golden rules:

a) Only do it in private.
b) Never use dangerous objects as sex toys
– e.g. glass bottles or anything sharp, dirty
or likely to break or get stuck inside you.

How boys do it:

For many boys, masturbation is a major
hobby. They touch their privates every time
they pee, so it's a small leap to give
themselves a hand-job. How? Most boys
hold their penis and rub it rhythmically until
they ejaculate. Like girls, some feel guilty
about it, but there's no need.

Q What's an orgasm (coming, having a climax)?

It's a series of little muscular spasms that
gives you a feeling of fantastic sexual
pleasure. It normally happens when your
genitals are stimulated during masturbation
or sex. When it happens, your heart beats
faster, the sensation spreads through your
body and you may feel as if you're floating.
Orgasms build to a peak then ebb away
after a few seconds, leaving you relaxed
and possibly sleepy. In boys, orgasm ends
in ejaculation.

Q When my boyfriend nibbles my ear, it really turns me on – how come?

Ears are erogenous zones! An erogenous zone is any part of the body that's sexually sensitive to touch – which includes being nibbled, kissed, stroked, licked, squeezed or tickled with a feather, if that's what turns you on. Different girls have different places where they like to be touched.

Q What's heavy petting (foreplay, touching up)?

It's sexual kissing and touching and can include kissing with tongues, him touching your breasts, touching each other's genitals or "dry humping" (boy-speak for rubbing against each other as if you're having sex, only with all your clothes on). This kind of touching creates feelings of intense pleasure and a desire to have sex.

WARNING!

When you're all loved-up like this, it's very hard to stop. If you're not ready to have sex or don't want to for whatever reason, make it clear to your partner from the beginning. If you forget, get carried away or change your mind, you can still say no to sex at any stage.

Crap things boys say to get you into bed

But I really love you.
(So why's he putting pressure on you like that?)

It'll prove how much you love me.
(He'd say the same if he wanted one of your crisps.)

If you don't want me, I know a girl who does.
(OK, bye!)

I can't wait for ever.
(Oh, please! He's known you 5 minutes!)

It'll prove you're not frigid.
(What – is he a doctor or something?)

I won't tell a living soul.
(Except all his mates.)

I'll dump you if you don't.
(He's dumped already, right?)

But my balls will turn blue!
(Good – they'll match his video collection.)

Q What's sexual intercourse?

Sexual intercourse is when a man puts his penis inside a woman's vagina and slides it in and out until he ejaculates. It can take over an hour or a few seconds.

Q Does losing your virginity hurt?

Some girls feel little or no pain, but it can be a bit sore if you have a tight or unbroken hymen (the thin layer of skin covering the vaginal opening). You may also bleed slightly. Also, if you are tense or nervous, your vagina will be tighter and dryer. Try using a lubricant like KY Jelly (from the chemist – often near the condom display) and take things slowly. The next time will be less painful.

Q What's oral sex?

Licking, sucking or kissing someone's genitals. When it's done to a guy, the proper word is fellatio (feh-lay-shee-oh). Slang expressions are Giving Head, Going Down On or giving a Blow Job. When it's done to a girl, it's called cunnilingus (cunny-ling-gus). Slang expressions are Licking Out, Eating and Going Down On.

Q What's anal sex?

Putting an erect penis, finger or other object up your bum hole (anus). The tissues inside the rectum can be easily damaged, so any activity in this area should be very gentle. Anal sex is highly risky because it may cause bleeding, and blood can carry diseases. Use a condom and never put anything that's been up your bum into your mouth or vagina.

GET THIS!
Many of us are virgins when we get married.

Other names for sexual intercourse (rudest last)

What Granny calls it:

doing it   having it awa[y]

how's your father

you-know-what

making whoopee   a bit of the other

What your mum calls it:

making love   having sex

sleeping with

intercourse

going to bed with

What the vicar calls it:

copulating   mating

conjugal right[s]

fornicating

consummating marriage vow[s]

What boys call it:

fucking

shagging   screwing

knobbing   giving her one

getting laid   poking

THE 3 Ps – 3 things every girl should know before she has sex

POLICE: In Britain, it is illegal to have sex if you're under 16. The law is there to protect under-age kids from abuse, and anyone caught having sex with someone under 16 could be charged.

PREGNANT: If you don't use contraception, you could get pregnant. Make sure you know how to use it and what to do if it fails (see pages 72–75).

POX: You could catch an STD (sexually transmitted disease). It's not very romantic, but there are some serious diseases that can be caught by having sex with someone who is infected. Some STDs don't produce symptoms for months, which means you could have a disease, not know you've got it and pass it on to someone else. The best way to protect yourself and your partner is to use a condom every time you have sex.

Sexually transmitted diseases

What	How
CHLAMYDIA	Vaginal sex/touching genitals then touching your eyes
GENITAL HERPES Type 1: sores on the nose/mouth Type 2: sores on genitals/anus	Kissing; oral, vaginal or anal sex
GENITAL WARTS Small fleshy growths that grow near genitals/anus	Contact with genitals vaginal, anal or oral sex
GONORRHOEA (CLAP)	Vaginal, anal or oral sex
HIV AND AIDS HIV = Human Immunodeficiency Virus, which attacks the immune system. An infected person is known as HIV positive but may stay well for years before they develop AIDS. AIDS = Acquired Immune Deficiency Syndrome, which is a collection of illnesses/conditions that occur when the body is weakened by HIV.	Vaginal, anal or oral sex
HEPATITIS B Viral infection of the liver – more infectious than HIV	Sexual contact; through blood or saliva with blood in

mptoms	Cure
t women won't notice any but may e vaginal discharge, frequent or painful ing, stomache ache, pain during sex, gular bleeding, sore eyes.	Antibiotics (if not treated, can lead to infertility)
ng, tingling around mouth/genitals. ers develop which burst and leave ful sores. Possible flu-like symptoms. ing this time, all sexual contact ild be avoided.	NONE – attacks can re-occur at any time
ie can be almost invisible, others mble tiny cauliflowers. May itch. cause cancer in women, so best ted on discovery.	Podophyllin (a paint-on solution), freezing or laser treatment
always. Sometimes painful ing/sore throat. A rash can develop ch affects the nervous system.	Penicillin
: night sweats, fever, lack of energy, rhoea, weight loss, thrush, herpes, dry and rashes, mouth ulcers and ding gums. S: breathing problems, eyesight blems, brain problems, cancer.	NONE – although therapies and medical research are advancing all the time
of energy and appetite, fever, diced skin, yellowing of whites of , pale poo, dark wee, abdominal pain.	NONE – but some recover after rest

Q Help! I'm in love but I'm not sure whether to have sex with my boyfriend.

You love him – he loves you. You've gone past first base, had a steamy snog and no doubt a case of the wandering hands. It's time to ask yourself some serious questions:

1. DO YOU HONESTLY BELIEVE YOU ARE BOTH IN LOVE?

If he's not in love with you, he could break your heart like a cracker biscuit. If you're only doing it because all your mates have, don't! You only lose your virginity once – shame if you can't remember where you put it!

2. CAN YOU TALK TO HIM ABOUT SEX?

If you end up giggling and avoiding the issue, you're not ready – that's fine. If you're not confident enough to tell him to stop, avoid being alone with him for now. Give it time.

3. DO YOU TRUST HIM?

You need to be able to trust him 100%. Sex makes us vulnerable, physically and emotionally. It's normal to feel nervous the

Shall we?

first time, but if your partner frightens you, suggests things you don't want to do or doesn't respect you, say no before you get hurt.

4. HAVE YOU DISCUSSED CONTRACEPTION?

You really have to talk about this – he may assume you've sorted it and are on the pill. You may think he'll bring condoms, but what if he doesn't? If neither of you is mature enough to sort out decent contraception, who's going to be responsible for the baby?

5. HOW LONG HAVE YOU KNOWN HIM?

Love (and lust) can happen at first sight, but it's best to get to know the guy for a while before you jump into bed.

6. DO YOU KNOW HOW TO HAVE SAFE SEX?

Using condoms is the best protection against STDs. If you don't know your boyfriend's sexual history and he refuses to wear a condom, refuse to have sex with him – it sounds mean, but giving someone a poxy disease is worse.

IF YOU DO DECIDE TO HAVE SEX, plan ahead to make it safe and special. Find somewhere private, take your time and don't expect too much first go. It takes two to tango (and you'll know when you've been tango-ed).

PREGNANCY

To get pregnant, all you need to do is have sex without using contraception. If your boyfriend is fertile (chances are, he is) and you're fertile (and you could be ovulating even before your first period) it's possible to get pregnant the very first time you have sex – you can never be too careful. Around 90,000 teenage girls get caught out every year in Britain.

HOW PREGNANCY (conception) HAPPENS

1 When a man ejaculates inside a woman's vagina, hundreds of millions of sperm cells are deposited near the cervix.

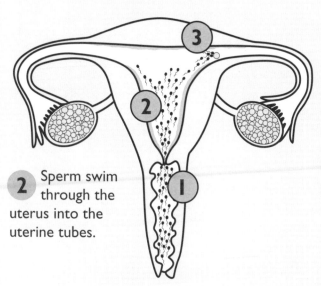

2 Sperm swim through the uterus into the uterine tubes.

3 If there's an ovum (egg) in one of the tubes, sperm cluster around it and one may join it. This is conception. Together, ovum and sperm make one new cell, which develops into a baby.

Don't believe the myths!

You can get pregnant if the man withdraws before he comes...

You can get pregnant the first time you have sex...

You can get pregnant if you have sex standing up...

You can get pregnant if you have sex during your period...

You can get pregnant if you pee straight after sex...

You can get pregnant if you don't have an orgasm...

IMPOSSIBLE! We were standing up!

How not to get pregnant

Lots of girls want to be mums one day but most would rather start a family when they're good and ready. You have a choice: if you don't want to get pregnant, you can either say no to sex for now, or decide to use contraception.

Birth control methods

What	How
CONDOM (johnny, rubber) A thin latex covering that fits over the erect penis (disposable)	It catches sperm ar stops it entering th vagina. 86% effectiv used properly.
DIAPHRAGM/CERVICAL CAP A washable latex dome that fits inside the vagina and covers the cervix. Check for holes!	Used with spermici it kills sperm/preve them entering cerv 80–90% effective.
SPERMICIDE A cream, gel, foam or pessary inserted into the vagina/used with other methods to make them more effective	Contains chemicals that kills sperm. 72–94% effective.
BIRTH CONTROL PILL A pill that controls hormones. (Two main types with different dosages.) Not advised for smokers.	One contains progesterone, whic prevents ovulation. The other contains progestin, which makes the uterus unsuitable for an eg 95–99% effective.
IUD A plastic/copper device that fits inside the uterus	Prevents egg from settling in uterus. 98–99% effective.

here	Pros	Cons
eaply from ps. Free from ily-planning ics and doctors.	The best prevention against STDs except for saying no	Can split/tear. You have to interrupt sex to put it on.
ey have to itted at the ily-planning ic/doctor's.	Doesn't interrupt sex as you can put it in 1–2 hours before	Can be fiddly to put in. Must stay in place 6–8 hours after sex.
emist, doctor's	Reduces the risk of pregnancy when used with other methods	Not reliable used alone. Can be messy. Can cause skin allergy.
prescription	Very effective against pregnancy. Possibly lighter, less painful periods.	You must take it regularly. Can cause side-effects: nausea, headache, bloating, weight gain, breast tenderness and depression.
ey have to fitted at the ily-planning ic/doctor's.	Can be kept in place for years. Can't feel it.	Can cause infection. Not recommended if you haven't had children.

EARLY SIGNS OF PREGNANCY

These start about 2 weeks after conception and can include a missed period, morning sickness and tender breasts.

Missing a period might not mean you're pregnant, but if you've had sex without using contraception and you're late, do a pregnancy test. Kits can be bought at the chemist. They're easy to use and accurate if you use them properly. If you are pregnant, don't kid yourself it isn't happening.

Worst Case Scenario
HELP! I think I may be pregnant.
I don't know what to do.

If you forget to take the pill or a condom splits, you can get "morning after" pills from the doctor, family-planning clinic or over the counter at the chemist. As long as you take them within 72 hours of having sex, they usually stop you getting pregnant. These are for emergency use only – never use them as a method of contraception.

If you've left it too late and a pregnancy test indicates that you really are pregnant, don't despair. You're not the first girl it's happened to and you won't be the last. You're not dirty, evil or a slag. Accidents happen to women much older and wiser than you. Don't be scared of telling your mum – most mums will do everything they can to help their pregnant daughters. If she blows a fuse, you can bet it's because she blames herself in some way. (Nuts, but there it is.) She'll also be worried for you. If you really can't face your parents yet, you still need to tell someone fast because apart from a cuddle, you'll need help and advice to decide what to do next.

People you could talk to:

Mum or Dad; one of Mum's friends that you trust; a close relative (a favourite auntie, maybe); a teacher you really like; your doctor; the school nurse; your boyfriend. There are lots of people who will help you and not judge you.

What are your options?

- ✪ You can keep the baby.
- ✪ You can have it adopted.
- ✪ You can have an abortion.

Whatever you decide, each option has consequences that will affect your life in the future. Don't try and go it alone.

BEING A TEEN MUM

Bringing up a baby is really hard work. It's even harder if you're in your teens, you're single and the pregnancy wasn't planned. Some girls cope brilliantly (it's not all doom and gloom!) but others have a tough time – here are some of the reasons they give:

✳ You lose your freedom – babies need care 24/7, leaving you little time to go out.

✳ Boredom, loneliness and depression.

✳ You may have to survive on benefits – and babies and childcare are expensive.

✳ Your studies may have to go on hold.

✳ Where will you live? Most teenage mums don't end up living with the baby's father.

✳ Single mums have trouble finding boyfriends – it's harder to meet Mr Right.

WHAT'S AN ABORTION?

ABORTION IS AN OPERATION to end a pregnancy. It's sometimes also called a termination. It involves removing the developing foetus from the womb by suction, scraping or with medication, depending on how advanced the pregnancy is. An abortion must always be performed by a registered doctor in a clinic or hospital – abortion clinics can be found in the telephone directory but it's best to be referred by your GP. Before an abortion is allowed two doctors must agree that having a baby would harm the mother's physical or mental health, or that it would be disabled.

In Britain, abortion is legal up to the 24th week of pregnancy but it's safest to have the operation in the early stages of pregnancy (within the first 3 months). Many doctors are unwilling to perform late abortions, for moral and medical reasons.

Having an abortion can screw you up emotionally – while some girls just feel relieved that it's over, others have regrets and need support. If you're not sure whether to go ahead or not, ask to speak to a counsellor and find out as much as you can about the procedure.

SEXUAL ABUSE

Sex with someone you love can be fantastic – but sex is only good if you want it to happen. Few girls get through life without some boy trying it on – it can be upsetting, but it's often to do with the boy being immature. A sharp remark and a firm "NO!" should stop him.

The much nastier threat comes from pervy adults who use their power to make you do intimate stuff you don't want to do. The person could be a stranger or someone you know, like a neighbour or a relative. Whoever they are, there's *no way* they should be doing it. It's illegal for anyone to force you to have sex, touch you against your will or make unwanted sexual remarks. If you're under 16 it's even more serious.

If it happens, tell an adult you trust to make sure it stops. If your mum can't deal with it, tell your teacher. Don't be frightened to tell, even if you've promised not to. You've done nothing wrong – *they* have! Get help fast.

SAFETY TIPS FOR STREETWISE CHICKS

✪ Walk with friends whenever you can – there's safety in numbers.

✪ If you're walking any distance on your own, wear shoes you can run in.

✪ Avoid alleys, underpasses, stairwells and multi-storey car parks at night and stay in well-lit, busy areas. Don't take short-cuts through woods, fields or parks.

✪ Know where you're going – if you act lost, you're an easy target.

✪ Never hitch lifts – even in company.

✪ Stay away from the kerb. If a stranger kerb-crawls you, don't talk to him.

✪ Don't wear headphones – you won't hear anyone coming up behind you.

✪ Never give out your real name, address, phone number or school to anyone over the Internet, even if they seem genuine.

✪ If you're followed or approached, go to the nearest house/shop or stop a female passer-by. Tell them what's wrong and ask them to call the police or your parents. Incidentally, if you just scream for help people tend to ignore you – calling "fire" or "rape" is more likely to get attention.

IT SOMETIMES seems like everyone is having sex or talking about it. When you're young, the subject may seem so gross that you never want to go there. But sex isn't all about diseases and unwanted babies. Good, loving sex never feels smutty, slutty or scary. Sex with a partner who loves and respects you is fantastic! It makes you feel wanted. It makes you feel good. And hey, it's fun! Yes, be careful. Yes, know the facts. Then, when you feel ready and old enough and you're truly, madly, deeply in love, lie back and enjoy it! Or swing off the chandelier together. Whatever turns you on.

INDEX

Where Next? For further advice, check out:
ChildLine: 0800 11 11 • www.childline.co.uk
Being Girl: www.beinggirl.co.uk
FPA (sexual health): www.fpa.org.uk
London Lesbian & Gay Switchboard: 020 7837 7324